To Cynthia

"[The] process of extracting the cosmic from the mundane is what animates all Nelson's work, and especially his domestic dramas set in Rhinebeck. I can't think of another body of theatrical work that has addressed so immediately, in such quotidian detail, the way we live now. A sense of the ephemerality of life, and the preciousness of its most prosaic elements, has pervaded all of these plays. But it assumes a special urgency in this hourlong [play]... Talking has never felt more essential. Many of the subjects have a ripe familiarity. The matinee-idol ascension of Governor Andrew M Cuomo is a topic. Others are closer to home, including the newly fraught act of grocery shopping; the difficulties of conducting a job remotely; the worries and resentment of younger relatives who feel their adult lives have been blighted just as they are beginning; and, most soberingly, the loss of friends to the virus.

But the main theme here is that these people are in conversation, which is in itself an assertion of human life, of community, of our ability to reciprocally confirm one another's identities.

The theatrical impulse—to celebrate and capture a moment in real time as it passes—is so strong here that, I actually felt I was attending a play."
Ben Brantley, *The New York Times*

"Nelson creates the first original internet play that deftly responds to the form, this family and the times. Call it Zoom Theater, and call it terrific. In WHAT DO

WHAT DO WE NEED TO TALK ABOUT?

The Apple Family:
Conversations on Zoom

Part One:
A Pandemic Trilogy

Richard Nelson

BROADWAY PLAY PUBLISHING INC
New York
www.broadwayplaypub.com
info@broadwayplaypub.com

Cover photo by permission of The New York Shakespeare Festival d/b/a The Public Theater ("NYSF")

First edition: November 2020
I S B N: 978-0-88145-887-9

Book design: Marie Donovan
Page make-up: Adobe InDesign
Typeface: Palatino

WE NEED TO TALK ABOUT? —indeed all his Apple plays, Nelson shows that a miniaturist can create a mural, encompassing a breathtaking expanse, without losing the attention to detail that is so essentially human."
Frank Rizzo, *Variety*

"Theater in exile does not mean a world without 'theater'. That much is clear after the premiere on Wednesday of Richard Nelson's riveting new drama, WHAT DO WE NEED TO TALK ABOUT? In 60 lyrical minutes, author-director Nelson and five stage-vet actors show us how potently a digital conferencing platform can work as a space for a play....

This is indeed one of the most Chekhovian of Nelson's Rhinebeck plays, a cycle that also includes other families, talking together on other nights. On this night, the poignant philosophy of UNCLE VANYA's Sonia echoes in a viewer's ears, the fervent one that says despite adversity: Yes, we will go on."
Peter Marks, *The Washington Post*

WHAT DO WE NEED TO TALK ABOUT? was first produced by the Public Theater (Oskar Eustis, Artistic Director, Patrick Willingham, Executive Director) on the Public's dedicated YouTube Channel on 29 April 2020, with the following cast and creative contributors:

RICHARD APPLE .... Jay O Sanders
BARBARA APPLE .... Maryann Plunkett
MARIAN APPLE .... Laila Robins
JANE APPLE .... Sally Murphy
TIM ANDREWS .... Stephen Kunken
BENJAMIN APPLE *(voice)* .... Jon DeVries

Director .... Richard Nelson
Production stage manager .... Teresa Flanagan
Technical director .... Ido Levran
Production manager .... Jeff Harris
Company manager .... Rebecca Sherman

CHARACTERS & SETTING

RICHARD APPLE, *lawyer in the state's Governor's office; lives in Albany.*

BARBARA APPLE, *his sister, high school English teacher.*

MARIAN APPLE, *his sister, elementary school teacher.*

JANE APPLE, *free-lance writer for local magazines.*

TIM ANDREWS, JANE's *partner, manager of a local restaurant and part-time actor.*

Time: A day in mid-April, 2020. 7:30-9 P M

Place: Various simultaneous locations, Rhinebeck, New York

Four computer screens:

BARBARA *and* RICHARD *appear in the living room of* BARBARA APPLE's *house on Center Street, Rhinebeck, where* RICHARD *has been staying for five weeks.*

JANE *appears in the living room of her and* TIM's *apartment on Livingston Street, Rhinebeck.*

TIM *appears in the bedroom in his and* JANE's *apartment on Livingston Street.*

MARIAN *appears in the living room of her house on Platt Street, Rhinebeck.*

NOTE

I use a single quotation mark to notate when the character is paraphrasing, and double quotation marks when the character is actually reading from a source.

1.
Why the Long Face?

(On one screen, BARBARA *sits waiting. She looks at herself in the screen, plays with her hair, etc.)*

(Second screen, an empty living room.)

(After a moment, JANE *appears on the second screen.)*

JANE: Sorry... *(She has a cup of tea. She also has a plate of cookies by the computer.)* What were you saying?

BARBARA: A horse walks into a bar. And the horse asks for a drink.

JANE: Who does he ask?

*(*RICHARD *appears behind* BARBARA, *he has just come into the room.)*

RICHARD: What kind of drink?

BARBARA: It doesn't matter.

JANE: *(Explains to* RICHARD*)* Barbara's telling a joke.

RICHARD: *(Incredulous) Barbara* is telling a joke??

JANE: Let her tell it.

BARBARA: *(Answering* RICHARD*)* A whiskey. I don't know. It doesn't matter. And—

RICHARD: Where did you get the joke?

BARBARA: The nice guy at the hospital, who gets you your car...

RICHARD: He told you a joke, why?

BARBARA: He's being friendly. He's a volunteer.

JANE: *(Sipping her tea, getting her attention)* Barbara… So the horse…

BARBARA: Orders a drink. A whiskey. And then the horse orders a second whiskey. And then a third.

RICHARD: Okay.

BARBARA: And the bartender—he ordered it from the bartender.

RICHARD: I think we'd figured that out.

BARBARA: Jane asked. *(Continues)* So the bartender, he says, 'why the long face?' *(She smiles, pleased with herself. Then explaining:)* Horses have long… They can't do anything about it. It's how they are…

(TIM appears on a screen from a bedroom.)

TIM: I'm here. Am I the last one? Sorry.

JANE: Marian's not on yet.

RICHARD: Why are we not surprised?

TIM: I was talking to my daughter.

JANE: She okay?

TIM: Yeh… You know.

RICHARD: Barbara was telling us a joke, Tim.

TIM: *(Incredulous)* Barbara?

RICHARD: From the man who helps you out of the hospital—.

BARBARA: *(Over this)* Gets your car.

TIM: I wouldn't want that job now.

BARBARA: *(To TIM)* How are you feeling?

TIM: I don't know. I'm fine. It's just a bit of fever. I don't have the cough…

BARBARA: Take care of yourself.

RICHARD: *(To* BARBARA*)* So Jane's locked him in the bedroom.

JANE: I have… *(To* TIM*)* The graduation's off?

TIM: They haven't announced that yet. The prom's cancelled. Are you eating? What are you eating?

JANE: Just cookies….

BARBARA: You're in the same house. And this is now how you two talk to each other? On this…?

TIM: She also shouts at me through the bedroom door.

JANE: I don't shout… It's a thick door.

TIM: Barbara, we have one bathroom…Jane, are we eating while we're talking? I haven't eaten… I'm hungry… *(To the others)* I'm not allowed in the kitchen…

JANE: *(Getting up)* You want cookies?

TIM: No.

JANE: *(As she goes)* I'll see what we have…

TIM: Have you eaten, Richard?

RICHARD: *(Getting up)* I'm making us dinner. Hold on. Tim, Barbara's let me make her dinner! *(He goes)*

TIM: You look good. We're glad you're home.

BARBARA: I'm sorry you're not feeling well.

TIM: We closed the bistro….

BARBARA: I figured.

TIM: We gave it a shot with the take-out. *(Smiles)*

BARBARA: What's funny, Tim?

TIM: What we should have done, if we could have… Maybe the Beekman could still do this.

BARBARA: What?

TIM: There's an inn up in Lakeville? They closed the inn but they also have a restaurant, so they could keep doing take-out, and the restaurant put on its website, for every order we'll give away a free roll of toilet paper!

BARBARA: Were they hoarding—?

(RICHARD *returns, having heard this:*)

RICHARD: They're an inn, Barbara. With no guests. So they have toilet paper. He told me this.

TIM: *(Over the end of this)* Within three hours they had six hundred take-out orders! If only we had toilet paper, we'd still be in business…

(JANE *appears:*)

JANE: *(To* TIM*)* There's the chili you made last Wednesday…

BARBARA: Who are you talking to?

RICHARD: Tim.

TIM: It'll still be good.

JANE: *(Over this to* TIM*)* You think you were sick then? If you do, then you can have it all…

TIM: I don't know.

JANE: I'll give it to you then. *(As she goes)* You want bread? *(She is gone.)*

TIM: *(He calls off.)* Bread would be good!

(MARIAN *comes on:*)

MARIAN: Am I the last one? Hi Barbara, you look great. Richard. Hi Tim. Where's Jane?

RICHARD: She's getting Tim his food. She sets it outside the bedroom door.

MARIAN: Good idea. Be safe.

BARBARA: Hi Marian…I like the scarf…

MARIAN: I got dressed up for this.

RICHARD: I didn't…

MARIAN: *(Over this, to* BARBARA*)* You must have stories… *(Suddenly gets up)* You're drinking wine. Let me get a glass of wine… Hold on. Don't say anything interesting… *(She goes.)*

BARBARA: *(Calls to* MARIAN*)* I'm still on antibiotics.

TIM: *(Calls)* Jane! Could I have wine?!!

*(*BARBARA *gets up.)*

BARBARA: Excuse me…

RICHARD: What do you need?

BARBARA: Nothing that you can do for me, Richard… *(She goes.)*

RICHARD: *(To* TIM*)* The bathroom…

TIM: I guessed… She looks okay. She's been lucky.

RICHARD: They've tested her twice. And she's free.

TIM: Jane said.

RICHARD: I keep taking my temperature.

TIM: How's work?

RICHARD: The state of New York is still…I guess it's functioning…I'm trying. Doing my small part.

TIM: From home.

RICHARD: From Barbara's home.

TIM: Good. *(Then. Stunned)* Andrew Cuomo…

RICHARD: I know. I know. Everyone is surprised. Who would have believed it?

TIM: *(Amazed)* There's a good side to him… Who knew?

RICHARD: I've skyped with a few guys in our office. Their wives are saying— 'what have you been complaining about all these years?' 'You come home crying….' 'He's a nice guy…' *(Laughs)* Some things you can't explain. *(Short pause)* So you're going to be staying in that little spare bedroom for a while…

TIM: I am. The dog gets to go back and forth. We share him.

RICHARD: That's nice.

TIM: For the dog.

(MARIAN returning:)

MARIAN: *(Sitting back down with her wine)* Their cat stays with Jane…

TIM: The neighbors have kids, you hear them through that wall. They're up at six in the morning…

RICHARD: You only have the one bathroom. What do you do?

TIM: *(Shrugs)* I shout out, so Jane and the cat can run to the other side of the living room. And then I wipe down everything after, you know, with… And I think Jane then wipes it all down again…

(BARBARA returning:)

BARBARA: What did I miss?

(Fade out.)

2.
Grocery Shopping.

(A short time later; JANE *isn't back; on her screen: an empty living room.)*

*(*MARIAN, BARBARA, RICHARD *and* TIM *in the middle of a conversation)*

MARIAN: Barbara, I talked to her this morning, and she just sounded scared…

RICHARD: Can she hear? Jane?? Jane?

BARBARA: She's not there.

TIM: *(Over this)* I hear her in the kitchen. I think she's heating up my chili.

MARIAN: *(To BARBARA)* Tim's been doing all the shopping

TIM: Not now I can't.

MARIAN: No, of course not. But you've been doing the shopping all month, she said. And she hasn't been out? I didn't know that, Richard. Did you?

RICHARD: I sort of knew. I guessed.

MARIAN: *(To TIM)* Except for walks, right? And then mostly into the cemetery where no one is...

BARBARA: You walk in the cemetery now?

RICHARD: The Mills Mansion, Vanderbilt, Poet's Walk—they're all packed now, Barbara.

MARIAN: The New Yorkers are here.

BARBARA: They've been here...

MARIAN: Even more now.

RICHARD: *(Over this, to BARBARA)* We should walk in the cemetery...

TIM: No one's there....

RICHARD: Perfect.

MARIAN: Barbara, now Jane's going to have to go out and do the shopping...

TIM: She's already telling me, you can't eat this, Tim, you can't eat that. Like we're rationing...

MARIAN: She's scared...

TIM: I blow my nose and she calls through the door: how many tissues are you using?

RICHARD: It's because she doesn't want to go out to the grocery store.

BARBARA: You should only use one if you can, Tim.

JANE: *(As she appears)* Your chili and wine are outside the door... You talking about me? What are you saying.... Tim?

TIM: I'm getting my dinner. *(He disappears for a moment.)*

JANE: *(Calls off)* Throw away the napkins in there. Don't leave them on the tray... *(To the others)* We're working out a lot stuff... What were you talking about?

MARIAN: We were talking about shopping.

JANE: Oh god... I'll go. I'm going to go. What did Tim say?

MARIAN: Jane, I get there now just before six.

BARBARA: Why?

RICHARD: They have older people's hours. Starting at six. You have to be old.

JANE: I'm old.

BARBARA: Is she old enough?

MARIAN: I think Tops started that after you went into the hospital, Barbara.

JANE: Is it better then? Is anyone there?

RICHARD: At six?

MARIAN: It's packed with old people. I hate going.

JANE: Fuck!

MARIAN: I went the other day, god knows what I looked like—

BARBARA: I'm sure you looked just fine, Marian. It's a grocery store. In a pandemic.

MARIAN: I had my blue mask that I made out of pajamas, my ski cap with the pom poms to cover my hair, and that scarf a friend bought me from Paris for an extra layer. You know the one. Over much of my face... My glasses are steaming up, my scarf's half off, my hat's slipping down. I don't want to touch my face... I can't do that. I must have looked like a crazy person.

BARBARA: I doubt if anyone noticed, Marian.

MARIAN: I think they did.

JANE: I'm sure you looked fine.

RICHARD: Why not Hannaford? I like it better. The fruits and vegetables. Not any more crowded...

MARIAN: Look—our brother, the shopper.

RICHARD: I shop. In Albany, I live alone. I cook. I clean. What are you talking about?

MARIAN: You eat out like four times a week. You told me. Jane, Tops is just as good. And it's closer. Yesterday I had a couple real victories. Who knew? Sweet sausage. Barbara, there's a *Times* recipe...

BARBARA: *I* showed you that, Marian.

(RICHARD *is going away.*)

MARIAN: Where are you going, Richard? *(To* BARBARA*)* Did you?

(RICHARD *is gone.*)

BARBARA: He's made dinner. The whole thing. Wouldn't let me near the kitchen...I'm being spoiled. I feel like a queen. I like to be waited on.

JANE: That is so untrue, Barbara.

MARIAN: That's one big lie.

BARBARA: He wanted to cook, what could I do? What other victories? You were saying. At Tops.

MARIAN: The peanut butter I like. They had that, amazing.

TIM: *(Now eating)* Barbara, if you bring your own bags, you have to pack them yourself. They don't want to touch them.

MARIAN: I don't blame them.

TIM: No.

MARIAN: You'll be fine, Jane…

JANE: Chili warm enough?

TIM: It's great.

MARIAN: *(Over this)* Just stay away from people.

TIM: At least six feet.

JANE: How do you do that in a fucking aisle?

MARIAN: No pasta… Those shelves are completely stripped…Jane, you'll be fine. But be really careful…

BARBARA: *(Seeing* RICHARD*)* My god, did you make all that for me?

*(*RICHARD, *with a tray of food, appears.)*

BARBARA: Look at this, Jane, Marian… What our brother made…Chicken. Rice pilaf. Salad… Thank you… *(Holds up a plate)* Look. Look. Can you see? Our brother made this…

JANE: I'll bet your kitchen's a mess.

BARBARA: Is it?

RICHARD: I'm not going to answer that. You eating anything Marian?

MARIAN: I had a salad.

BARBARA: Marian, are you eating? Richard?

RICHARD: *(To* BARBARA*)* She says she eats. I've been asking.

MARIAN: Jane, it's not the hell you think it's going to be. Grocery shopping. It's not quite that... Almost.

BARBARA: Everybody have what they want? You need anything, Richard? I can get it.

RICHARD: I'm fine. I'm not hungry. Barbara, just stay where you are.

JANE: She can't do that.

BARBARA: *(Over this)* You will be hungry.

RICHARD: *(Over this)* Just eat, Barbara... Just eat... You're home...

(Fade out)

3.
Death and Retirement.

(BARBARA and RICHARD, JANE, TIM and MARIAN.)

(BARBARA and TIM eat their dinners. The others sip their wine. In the middle of a conversation:)

TIM: Older than me. I read he was sixty-nine. He looked younger.

BARBARA: *(To RICHARD)* Like our age.

RICHARD: Almost.

JANE: That's not old.

TIM: A really fine actor... And a great guy. Very funny. I did one play with him and a couple of readings. A really sweet man.

BARBARA: I'm sorry...

(TIM laughs.)

RICHARD: What, Tim?

TIM: Mark once told me a story about his parents.

RICHARD: What story?

TIM: When he was in his early twenties, I think. And so this in the early seventies, so the city is, it's a mess…

RICHARD: I remember that.

TIM: And he's in a play downtown, in the Village somewhere. Some hole in the wall, I think he said. And he's playing—it's an O'Neill play, set at sea, and Mark is this old Swedish sea captain. And Mark Blum is not Swedish, and he's like twenty-two years old and looks even younger. He said he wore a white beard that kept slipping down his neck. And one Saturday matinee his parents come in from New Jersey to see their son 'act'. In a 'professional' theater. They'd seen him in school plays. They're early… As parents always are for things like this.

JANE: We were like an hour early for Tim's daughter's school play…

TIM: So his parents take their seats. They're the first to arrive, of course. They wait, and wait until now it's fifteen minutes before the show is to start, and they're the only ones in the audience. And Mark's Mom, she turns to his Dad and says, 'Morty, if you love your son, you'll get some people in here.' And so Morty goes out into, I don't know, Christopher Street, and starts offering anyone five bucks to come and see his son in this play….

(Laughter)

BARBARA: Bless them.

TIM: Whenever we met, I'd look at Mark and say, 'Morty, if you love your son…' (He takes a bite. Short pause) He had asthma.

BARBARA: That's a nice way to remember your friend.

JANE: It is.

TIM: The theater, it's been... My actor friends... They tell me it's like they're just floating in the air. One said, it's like floating but you don't know if you're going to just crash to the ground and be dead or is something else going to happen... Are you suspended or falling...?

BARBARA: That must be hard.

TIM: Will there be theater?

RICHARD: At least you've got the restaurant business, that's working out well...

BARBARA: Richard...

RICHARD: If we can't laugh, Barbara...

TIM: Richard's right. If we can't laugh...

(Then)

JANE: Tim's friend's show will probably be cancelled.

TIM: At Bard. I'm not surprised.

RICHARD: What show?

JANE: He was going to stay with us. He gets some fee for housing, and he was going to pay us.

TIM: The spare bedroom... Right here.

JANE: A musical... His friend knows the director. The director did that—

TIM: *Oklahoma* last year. The radical one.

JANE: That started here—

BARBARA: At Bard.

JANE:—so the director is going to do another musical.

TIM: *Was*, Jane. It's not going to happen. And it's 'they', my friend uses 'they.'

JANE: I have such a hard time remembering that.

MARIAN: That started at Bard? *Oklahoma?*

RICHARD: Not the original.

MARIAN: I know that.

JANE: It's going to happen. Sometime. If not now. People will again need to be together sometime.

TIM: Will big groups of people want to sit tightly together in the same space for a couple of hours…? When will that happen again? How long will *that* take?

RICHARD: The first cough in the audience and who's listening to the play?

TIM: He's right.

JANE: You lose something like theater and you're basically saying, people—stay away from each other. So much more than going to a play gets lost…

RICHARD: A Russian friend of mine sent me some jokes going around over there. In Moscow… One has a politician giving a speech, 'Friends', he says, 'in these difficult days for our country we must keep as far as possible from each other.' *(Then)* Russian humor… *(Then)* And she sent this one, 'The people who buy toilet paper are incredible optimists, they think they will have food.'

JANE: That's not funny, Richard.

TIM: It's a joke. There's going to still be food, Jane… *(Then. To* JANE*)* Sometimes you go to such dark places.

MARIAN: You have to go to the grocery store, Jane. You'll live.

RICHARD: *(Continues)* I can work at home. I just need a computer. I don't need a crowd.

BARBARA: This is my home. Richard, you're working in my home.

RICHARD: You know what I mean. *(A joke)* 'You've made me feel at home.'

BARBARA: Bullshit.

JANE: She's been in the hospital.

RICHARD: Before that.

MARIAN: Is he paying rent?

JANE: Are you?

RICHARD: I'm staying with my sister. Jesus. And you teachers will have your jobs. You're even still teaching…

MARIAN: Not really. Second grade… But we're being paid.

BARBARA: I'm back tomorrow. On Zoom…

RICHARD: The Chronogram's still publishing—.

JANE: Online.

RICHARD: So Jane's all right.

JANE: There's no real way to distribute, the stores are closed. But I'm still writing…

MARIAN: Actually, I was thinking, this could be a good time, Jane. For style stories.

BARBARA: What do you mean?

MARIAN: The Chronogram stuff. Pictures of nice houses—barns turned into fancy jacuzzies.

JANE: We publish more than that.

MARIAN: That's what people read. And this is a good time to lose yourself in that sort of thing, no? Becky? You know, who does real estate.

BARBARA: I know Becky.

MARIAN: We talked the other day out in the street—ten feet apart. She was walking her dog. She said they now expect a boom—people buying up here.

TIM: Isn't there one already?

MARIAN: An even bigger one.

BARBARA: Why?

MARIAN: *(Over this)* People—like our brother here, they've seen how they can work from anywhere. And maybe they are liking that. And feeling safe.

RICHARD: Jesus.

BARBARA: *(To* RICHARD*)* Is that where we're headed?

MARIAN: She said she'd been overhearing people talk–.

BARBARA: About?

MARIAN: *(Over this)* —how there could be a big change in the city. People leaving. Even young people. People not wanting anymore to be so close to other people. That had been the attraction. Being close to people.

JANE: So they'll come up here?

MARIAN: And other places.

BARBARA: Then you better buy a house soon, Richard.

RICHARD: Barbara…

MARIAN: What are you talking about?

JANE: *(Same time)* What?

RICHARD: *(Standing up)* I'm going to pour myself some more wine…

BARBARA: Richard… you want to tell your sisters?

*(*RICHARD *moves away.)*

BARBARA: He doesn't.

JANE: Richard…?

MARIAN: What is this, Barbara?

BARBARA: He's just right there, Marian. *(Points)* He can hear… After I got home this afternoon, one of the first things he says to me is… *(To* RICHARD, *unseen)* You don't want to say… (*Then.* *To the sisters*) He says, "I'm going to retire."

MARIAN: I know nothing about this.

JANE: (*Same time*) What? I don't believe that.

RICHARD: (*Sitting back, with his wine*) I haven't told anyone. Barbara's the first.

MARIAN: Why is Barbara the first?

JANE: Marian.

BARBARA: (*Over this*) I'm the oldest.

MARIAN: Is this because of Cuomo?

RICHARD: It's not about Cuomo…

MARIAN: He's different now, Richard.

TIM: We talked about this.

MARIAN: I like him now.

RICHARD: It's not about Andrew Cuomo. I long ago learned how to deal with that. All that. It's great that he's found a voice. Good for him… It's nothing about that.

MARIAN: What's it about then?

(RICHARD *looks to* BARBARA; *she eats her dinner.*)

RICHARD: I've been here for five, six weeks now. And the last what, almost five, days, by myself. In *Barbara's* house…I've been working of course. But you start thinking…

JANE: You can commute to Albany from Rhinebeck. People do that. If it's Rhinebeck where you want to be.

RICHARD: It's not that, Jane.

BARBARA: Tell them… We talked… Tell them, Richard. They're your sisters.

JANE: And Tim.

RICHARD: I'm sixty-seven years old. That's after retirement age. Come on. I've put in my time…

MARIAN: You always said you'd never retire. You'd hang out your shingle somewhere…

BARBARA: He doesn't want to do that anymore.

RICHARD: You're disappointed in me.

JANE: What happened? What are you going to do?

RICHARD: Nothing happened, Jane. *(Then)* I can try and explain.

JANE: Please.

RICHARD: I was washing dishes…

MARIAN: What??

BARBARA: *(To* MARIAN*)* Sh-sh…

RICHARD: A few days ago. And looking out at Barbara's yard…I asked myself, why am I enjoying this so much?

MARIAN: Washing dishes? What are you talking about?

RICHARD: And so I analyzed it. Thought about it. And I suddenly realized, that in my job, with the Governor's office, *(Lists)* I argue for things, I write briefs, I file things, but it's like I'm living a circle… I get up, I do this work, and so forth… It's a fucking circle. But here I am washing dishes—this is just an example—and the pleasure this is giving me is, I suddenly realize, because it has a beginning, middle, and end. So, when I reach this end, I feel accomplished.

MARIAN: When you'd washed all the dishes.

RICHARD: Yeh. But it's not about dishes. I want to do something that I can finish. Does that make sense?

(Then)

MARIAN: You're not just overreacting to everything that's happened?

RICHARD: I'm not overreacting to anything. It's not even reacting, if it's anything it's 'learning from'...?

JANE: I need a glass of wine now... *(She gets up.)*

TIM: Jane, could I get some more wine?

JANE: *(Into the computer)* Richard don't say anything more, wait for me. *(As she goes, she shouts off:)* I'll leave the bottle outside the door! *(She goes away.)*

(Short pause)

RICHARD: I don't want to make this into a big thing.

BARBARA: It's not a big thing?

TIM: *(To say something)* Barbara, how's Richard's dinner?

BARBARA: Very nice. *(To RICHARD)* You're a cook.

RICHARD: There's plenty more... *(He starts to pick up her plate.)*

BARBARA: Leave it...I'm not finished. We're talking. Don't run away.

RICHARD: I wasn't running away.

BARBARA: Aren't you going to eat? You're just going to drink?

(JANE has come back with her wine.)

JANE: *(Sitting back down)* So you want to feel accomplished? You've held very responsible jobs.

RICHARD: When I die—

JANE: Marian, so this *is* all about what's happening. We're all scared, Richard.

MARIAN: He's scared.

RICHARD: The kids are taken care of...

MARIAN: Lily's still in college.

RICHARD: One more year. And I have saved for that. They're both fine. They took on no debt. And I have a good pension. Thank you New York State.

TIM: Hopefully not in stocks.

JANE: Not funny.

RICHARD: That's going to change, Tim.

MARIAN: *(Over the end of this)* What are you going to do?

BARBARA: That's what I asked him. He hasn't said… Have you thought about it?

RICHARD: Of course I have, Barbara.

BARBARA: You know you do make rash decisions.

RICHARD: When do I that? I'm incredibly methodical. I'm a lawyer—

BARBARA: *(for one example)* When you quit the clarinet. You just quit. You wouldn't even talk about it.

RICHARD: I was thirteen years old.

BARBARA: *That* was rash. You were good. *(To the sisters)* Wasn't he?

JANE: I don't know.

MARIAN: *(Same time)* I don't remember.

RICHARD: I'm thinking of following in Jane's footsteps.

JANE: What??

BARBARA: *(Same time)* What does that mean?

RICHARD: Trying to write, Barbara. Maybe history. I love history… That must be obvious. Maybe I'd start about our family.

BARBARA: Richard, Marian's doing that.

MARIAN: I am, Richard. You know that.

RICHARD: Maybe I can help, Marian, put things together.

MARIAN: What are you talking about?

RICHARD: Add things you haven't found. Make connections.

MARIAN: I think I'm doing that… You think I'm missing things?

RICHARD: I don't know.

MARIAN: Have you even read all the stuff I've been sending to you?

BARBARA: It's all very interesting, Marian.

MARIAN: He hasn't read it, has he?

JANE: I don't think so.

RICHARD: Okay. Some other history then. I love researching…

JANE: Have you really thought this out?

MARIAN: And are you going to retire here? In Rhinebeck?

RICHARD: Possibly.

BARBARA: That's why I brought up buying a house.

JANE: His last alimony check was in February. Maybe that has something to do with this?

RICHARD: That was a milestone, I admit. I do feel released… You know, even though I've been living alone, I don't spend that much time alone…I'm always busy. I volunteer for stuff. Boards. Like Barbara… I always try to be busy.

BARBARA: I don't mind being alone. I'm not scared of that.

RICHARD: It's not that I'm scared…

MARIAN: It's about the alimony.

RICHARD: *(Over this)* I've had time to think… That's all.

(Then)

MARIAN: Barbara's not going to cook for you, Richard.

RICHARD: I'm not asking that, for God's sake. I can cook. *(Gestures to* BARBARA's *plate)*

BARBARA: I don't think he's asking for that.

RICHARD: Of course I'm not.

BARBARA: Though he can always do my dishes. *(Smiles)*

MARIAN: Rhinebeck…I thought you were so worried about being smothered by your sisters.

RICHARD: I never said that, Marian. I never would say that.

JANE: Oh yes you did, Richard. You did.

MARIAN: You definitely did, Richard.

BARBARA: And right here in this house.

(Then:)

RICHARD: Let's talk about something else…

(Lights fade.)

4.
The Decameron.

(The same, a short time later)

BARBARA: I just spoke with my sub this afternoon; she says it's been okay. The students are liking the project. I think if they can connect all this, what they're feeling, *that* feeling, to something else…

TIM: Give it a context.

BARBARA: Especially in literature or art…I teach literature… Then I think a project like this can make it all more manageable. Help them with all this.

TIM: The pandemic.

BARBARA: So you're not hiding from, avoiding, but you're also not stuck in it.

RICHARD: Why the *Decameron*?

BARBARA: That's as a starting point.

JANE: You know what it's about.

RICHARD: Actually I don't…

JANE: Richard, it's people telling each other stories while they wait out a plague. Hundreds of years ago in Italy.

BARBARA: What's so interesting, is that these people, the characters, don't tell stories about plagues—instead they're about sex, intrigue, some are funny…some quite magical… We started before I got sick… The students wanted to tell each other about…

RICHARD: About what?

BARBARA: Things they needed to say. On their minds. *(Examples)* Their parents. Afraid for grandparents. While they're shut up in their homes… *(Then)* They were full of surprises. They always surprise me. That's why I don't want to retire, Richard, I'd really miss that. *(Continues)* Some just made up stories. Some told plots of T V shows they're watching.

JANE: Streaming.

BARBARA: And that's okay too. I think it makes you feel like you're doing something.

TIM: Telling stories.

BARBARA: So do we want to try this? We don't have to. The kids like it.

JANE: I'm in, Barbara.

TIM: Me too.

MARIAN: *(Over this)* Why not? So then who's first?

BARBARA: Richard, you good?

RICHARD: Sure…

BARBARA: Jane, maybe you can go first?

JANE: I'm the youngest.

MARIAN: That's why. You do what we tell you to.

RICHARD: God I wish, Marian…

JANE: Okay. Let me think…

MARIAN: You have something?

JANE: Let me think, Marian.

TIM: Jane, what about…?

JANE: What?

TIM: That novelist you've been…

MARIAN: Who's that?

JANE: I could do that. I could tell that. Sure. *(She gets up to go.)*

MARIAN: *(Over the end of this)* What's that?

JANE: Tim, where's my notebook…? *(She goes.)*

MARIAN: Where are you going…?

TIM: *(Calls)* It's in here, Jane, on your desk. *(He disappears.)*

JANE: *(Off)* Can you get it for me? But wipe it down. Wipe it down!

TIM: *(Off, shouts)* I'll put it outside the door!

(Then)

RICHARD: What's this about?

MARIAN: I have no idea. Some story? She's always researching something.

BARBARA: *(To* RICHARD*)* You sure you're okay?

RICHARD: Could be fun, Barbara…

MARIAN: Richard, you know, I'm sitting here thinking we are so lucky.

RICHARD: Why?

MARIAN: *(The answer)* Barbara.

BARBARA: Marian, come on.

MARIAN: We can say that, damnit.

RICHARD: We are.

MARIAN: You're home…

BARBARA: You know there are so many people who can't stay at home like this, who can't lock themselves up in their houses and apartments… *That's* why we're lucky…

JANE: *(Returning)* So I just tell the story?

BARBARA: Anything at all.

JANE: *(Wiping the book)* Hopefully it's not too boring.

TIM: *(Returning)* It's not.

RICHARD: And if it is, Marian will tell you, Jane.

MARIAN: What do you mean by that?

JANE: *(Her story)* I came across a novel, published anonymously in the fifties. It had been a huge success, a best seller. The writing compared to Henry James. As well as being scandalous. The woman at the center of the novel has a secret…

TIM: She's been telling me all about this…

JANE: When this character was fifteen, she began a sexual affair with her fifty year-old and very wealthy step-father. At this time, her mother, his wife, was in their house, up in her bedroom, dying.

BARBARA: When did you research this?

TIM: She works all the time, Barbara.

JANE: I want to write a piece about novels by women from the thirties, forties, fifties. Especially those forgotten.

TIM: Or 'lost'.

JANE: When this novel came out there was all kinds of speculation about who actually wrote this anonymous book. Even the rumor that it was Winston Churchill.

BARBARA: You're kidding.

JANE: Another Isak Dineson.

MARIAN: *Out of Africa.*

JANE: About six months after it's published, *The Times* 'unmasks' the anonymous author. She is a sixty-something American woman living in England: her name: Gladys Huntington. In her whole life she'd written one novel, while in her twenties—not good, actually terrible, and a couple of stories. Then in her sixties, she suddenly writes a critically acclaimed bestseller. That's surprising. Unmasked as its author, she's feted. There are parties for her, interviews in newspapers, and then about a year or so later, this woman, Gladys, kills herself…

BARBARA: Why?

JANE: I read a letter of Gladys' from around the time when she was being acclaimed. In this letter, Barbara, she calls herself 'worthless'.

BARBARA: Why?

TIM: Jane thinks she's uncovered why, Barbara.

JANE: I also happen to be researching another female novelist, one completely forgotten now, if she ever really was known. Helen Granville-Barker, very wealthy, and married to a famous English playwright. She wrote a number of novels which were never successful, though they were critically well received. Being so rich I don't think she cared about promoting them. Anyway, she dies in 1950, and she leaves a will, which I've come across, on-line...

TIM: Helen's will.

JANE: Her husband, the playwright, had already died. So in her will, she leaves some things to her lawyers and doctor and to a 'Gladys Huntington' —the same— it says right there in the will, Helen leaves Gladys her letters, and her papers...

TIM: Which of course would include any manuscripts.

JANE: Helen's own novels, and I've now read all of them, are written in a style very similar to the anonymous book now being attributed to Gladys Huntington.

RICHARD: You think this Gladys stole Helen's novel?

TIM: And then killed herself. Because she was guilty.

JANE: I don't know that for sure, Tim.

TIM: I think that's why.

JANE: I know you do.

RICHARD: That novel could have been with part of her papers...

MARIAN: (*Over the end of this*) There are a lot of authors with similar styles, Jane. Are you just guessing?

TIM: Tell her. It's incredible what she's putting together.

JANE: Marian, the stepfather in the book is named Carlos. Helen's Uncle was *Collis* Huntington.

TIM: One of the richest men in America. He owned a lot of railroads among other things.

JANE: When Helen was fifteen, Marian, Collis was—fifty. And at this time, Collis' wife—was in their home, up in her bedroom, dying...

TIM: Of course Collis/Carlos that's very close. Sounds similar. But Jane also learned—

JANE: —that when Collis Huntington bid at art auctions in New York, he bid under a code name, so people didn't know it was him and bid him up. His code name, Marian: 'Carlos'.

BARBARA: Just like in the book.

JANE: When the woman in the novel's brother arrives, he calls out to his sister, 'Nellie.' Her name up until then in the book has been 'Natalia'.

TIM: Jane's written to various libraries.

JANE: And they have sent me copies of Helen's own letters... One of these letters from the Huntington Library in California, is from a sixteen-year old Helen—to a cousin. In this letter, young Helen writes, "I want now to be called only 'Nellie'". *(Then)* Marian, I think this book is about Helen's own life.

TIM: Why she never published it.

JANE: Her secret life.

MARIAN: What's the name of the novel?

TIM: This is neat.

JANE: *Madame Solario.* Of course 'solario' means—exposed, like a solarium. Open to the world...

TIM: It's still in print with Glady's name on the cover.

BARBARA: So you're going to write about this?

JANE: Yes. Helen's forgotten, Barbara. And that doesn't seem right.

(Then)

BARBARA: Throughout all that, as you told that story, Jane, I did not once think about a pandemic!

RICHARD: Neither did I.

(Laughter)

TIM: Isn't that the point?

JANE: Marian.

MARIAN: I'm next?

RICHARD: Have you thought of something?

MARIAN: It's not as fantastic as that. Yes, Richard. It's a story about our family.

RICHARD: Something we know?

MARIAN: I don't think so.

JANE: Richard, *she's* been researching—

RICHARD: I know. I know.

*(*MARIAN *takes a sip of her wine:)*

MARIAN: I hadn't known anything about Paul.

TIM: Paul?

JANE: Dad's brother. Benjamin's brother.

MARIAN: It's like he was wiped off the earth...

RICHARD: That is true.

MARIAN: I tried all sorts of websites... No record of him marrying. No children. We know he left the family and moved to Texas.

RICHARD: For oil.

MARIAN: He was a wildcatter, Tim.

TIM: Really?

MARIAN: We never talk about Paul.

RICHARD: We don't know anything about—

BARBARA: Maybe she does. Have you been saving this?

MARIAN: In a way… *(Then)* A cousin of ours. A third cousin? I think we're related. She's been researching the Apple family as well. And our paths crossed on-line. She'd talked to, maybe her mother? I don't know. And she heard this story, which she passed along to me…. *(Then)* Sometime after the war, Grandpa and Paul got into a fight. No one ever knew what that fight was about. A girl? Someone Paul wanted to marry? Money? It's all speculation. Anyway, Grandpa and Paul fought, and Grandpa basically disowned him. Said he wanted nothing more to do with him. Paul then went away, everyone in the family lost contact. Now jump ahead to Grandpa's funeral. *(Then)* Barbara you would have been like six or seven, do you remember…?

BARBARA: Was I even there. Richard?

RICHARD: I don't remember.

MARIAN: Dad and Benjamin were of course there. Maybe Mom…

JANE: Probably.

MARIAN: And they all go back to Grandpa's… Grandma's dead. And the lawyer opens up Grandpa's will. *(To* JANE*)* Another story about a will, Jane. Barbara, you don't know this, right?

BARBARA: No.

RICHARD: No.

MARIAN: Opens up the will. 'So and so to Dad.' 'To Benjamin.' 'To friends.' 'To whomever, whatever…' A list. Very methodical.

RICHARD: That was Grandpa, right?

BARBARA: I don't know.

MARIAN: Then it comes to the very last thing. The lawyer reads, "And to Paul…" And everyone in that room stops breathing, silence, you could hear a pin drop, he reads "And to Paul—I leave one silver dollar. And I hope he chokes on it."

(Short pause as they take this in.)

TIM: Jesus… What were they fighting about?

BARBARA: We don't know.

JANE: I would love to know.

BARBARA: We'll never know…

MARIAN: I'm going to keep researching Paul… He can't have just vanished.

TIM: You think he's alive?

MARIAN: He'd be a hundred years old. I doubt it. But he must have left some trace of himself somewhere. We don't just vanish…

RICHARD: Are we sure about that?

MARIAN: You think we just vanish?

(Then)

BARBARA: Richard? Your turn.

MARIAN: You ready?

RICHARD: I'm ready…

MARIAN: You want to take some time and think about it?

RICHARD: *(Ignoring her)* Barbara, while you've been in the hospital these few days, I have been alone here in your house, and I have looked through your books. And I came across a book I'd loaned you years ago.

MARIAN: She doesn't give things back. She's bad about that.

JANE: You really are, Barbara.

BARBARA: I know… Anyway it stayed in the family…

RICHARD: *(Continues)* A biography of President Franklin Pierce that I bought in England years ago… I'd forgotten about it, so I read it again. It's very interesting. His was a totally failed presidency.

MARIAN: Oh I can't imagine such a thing.

TIM: That's relevant.

MARIAN: Tim, I can't watch him now. I just can't—

JANE: *(Over the end of this)* When could you, Marian?

BARBARA: *(Over this)* What's the story, Richard?

(Then)

RICHARD: There's one incident in the book, I'd forgotten it. Perhaps it didn't even happen, it's a story. About the first time a Japanese delegation announced a visit to Washington. No one from Japan had ever been there. That country had been closed and in advance of their coming they sent gifts to the President: silks, swords, vases, umbrellas, mats, jars, plants, and—a dog. A little yapping dog. A whole new different breed. 'What are we going to do with this stuff?' No one knew. The dog just ran around the White House, yapping and yapping. He was a nasty little dog. *(Then)* One day, President Pierce, who was—my size—after some strenuous meeting or something, everything was falling apart in his administration—he throws himself into an armchair—where the yapping dog has been napping—and he crushes it. He crushes their gift. And in just two days the delegation from Japan will arrive. *(Then)* 'Do we tell them the truth?' 'Do we find another dog?' No one had ever seen a dog like that. 'Do we find some flunky to blame?' 'Isn't that what we normally do?' Typical government stuff. That's what they do in Albany. Anyway, it was finally agreed to have the dog

stuffed… And twisted into a kind of 'sleeping pose.'
So that's what they did, and then they stick the dog in
a corner. The Japanese arrive, they all have a pleasant
meeting. And they leave. Later the American translator
returns and tells the President how impressed the
Japanese were. 'What impressed them?' he said.
'Getting that yapping dog to shut up!' They never
could.

MARIAN: That really happened?

RICHARD: Maybe… It's a story. It's history.

MARIAN: History usually has happened, Richard.

RICHARD: Not always… Not in Albany. *(Continues)*
When his presidency ended he was hated, Marian…
And *he* wasn't re-elected.

MARIAN: We can hope and pray. Fingers crossed.

JANE: Tim should be next. He hasn't had a turn. You
have something?

TIM: I do.

BARBARA: Tim?

JANE: *(Over this)* He always does.

TIM: You might be bored… Mine's about—surprise—
the theater…I can also talk about restaurants. That's
about it…

JANE: That's not true.

TIM: This week I was Skyping with Gideon, my
friend at Bard, and a writer friend of his. We're
commiserating about cancelling the play this
summer…

JANE: The musical.

TIM: They were trying to figure—how to do something.
To keep going… Do theater. Somehow. To just make
the point that we're not done. We're not finished.

(Then) So we quickly think of something like this. What we're doing. On Skype or Zoom, stream it or put it on YouTube. It's not the same of course, but it shows we're not giving up. So—what to put on? A play. I suggest maybe *Skin of Our Teeth*...

RICHARD: I don't know that...

TIM: Sort of about the end of the world.

MARIAN: Oh that's a good idea.

BARBARA: *(Explaining* MARIAN *to* TIM*)* She doesn't think it is.

TIM: I know, Barbara. *(Then)* Gideon's friend got talking about the play *The Cherry Orchard*... You know it...

RICHARD: Tell me again the story. I've never seen it.

MARIAN: *(Over the end of this)* I forget too.

TIM: A woman has an abusive husband, he dies, probably of drink and so she thinks she's suddenly freed and begins an affair. But right away tragedy strikes; her young son accidently drowns in the river. *(Then)* She's grief-stricken. Guilty as hell. She runs away, to punish herself, where she goes through hell. A few years go by, and she finds her way home again. That's when the play starts. At that time her estate and its cherry orchard are about to be sold at auction because certain debts haven't been paid. *(Then)* A simple solution to this is offered, and she and her brother ignore it. Usually when you see this play, Richard, she and the brother are portrayed as fading aristocrats who have their heads in the sand, oblivious to the social changes around them. Gideon's friend disagrees with this. It's simpler and far, far more complex and human than that, he says. *(Then)* Her problem is that she needs to heal from the tragedy of her son's death. But to heal she knows in her gut that she'll have to sell the estate and orchard, because they are irrevocably tied to her dead son. But selling feels like a profound disloyalty to that same son. So, here is her dilemma: she needs the estate sold, but *she* can't be the one to sell it. And so that's what happens: it's sold, but not by her, and by the end she is smiling, sleeping again… She is healing.

BARBARA: So it's all about healing…

TIM: And this I found so moving—maybe even more so now, I mean right now. He said, that this incredible play about the need to heal, the need to go on, was written by a man who at the time knew he was dying. Even on his deathbed he fought to keep going. How human is that? *(Pause)* Barbara's turn…

RICHARD: You have something?

BARBARA: When I was in the hospital…

RICHARD: You going to talk about that? Yourself?

BARBARA: I can talk about myself.

RICHARD: Not really…

BARBARA: When I was in the hospital… All alone. Watching the people there… The people working… Do you all remember almost ten years ago—Uncle Benjamin read a poem at the high school?

RICHARD: Anniversary of 9/11.

TIM: I was there.

JANE: I remember that.

RICHARD: Me too.

BARBARA: Remember the poem he read?

RICHARD: No.

BARBARA: I remembered sitting in here, in the living room with him, helping him prepare.

JANE: You were amazing.

BARBARA: I'm not asking for that. I bring it up because, in these 'prep' sessions I would sometimes record him. So I could play it back, be more objective, give him advice. I was pretty sure I hadn't thrown it out.

RICHARD: The recording?

BARBARA: I found it right away... One of the first things I did when I came home, Richard.

RICHARD: That's why you were in the basement?

BARBARA: So, can I play it for you...? That's my story... It's not the best recording, but you can hear him...

MARIAN: Benjamin...

(BARBARA *gets up.*)

BARBARA: It's on the table... (*She goes away for a moment.*)

JANE: I haven't heard his voice in a such a long time.

MARIAN: This was the year Evan died.

BARBARA: (*Sitting back down*) That's right. You okay with that?

MARIAN: Yeh...

(BARBARA *holds a small tape recorder:*)

BARBARA: Okay? Ready... (*She starts it.*) Wait... It's coming... You know I edited the poem... Shortened it for him...

BENJAMIN: (*On tape, reads*) "An old man...

BARBARA: (*Over this*) Here... Listen

BENJAMIN: "An old man ..."

BARBARA: Loud enough?

BENJAMIN: "bending..."

MARIAN: I can hear.

BENJAMIN: "I come among new faces,"

JANE: Benjamin!

BENJAMIN: "Years looking backward resuming in
  answer to
Children,"

JANE: I so remember this…

BENJAMIN: "Come tell us old man...

RICHARD: I can see him, Jane…

JANE: Me too…

BARBARA: *(Same time)* Me too…

BENJAMIN: "But in silence, in dreams' projections,
Bearing the bandages, water and sponge,
Straight and swift to my wounded I go,
Where they lie on the ground after the battle brought
  in,
where their priceless blood reddens the grass the
  ground...

JANE: Benjamin…

BENJAMIN: "Back on his pillow the soldier bends...
His eyes are closed, his face is pale, he dares not look
  on the bloody stump,
And has not yet look'd on it.
I dress a wound in the side, deep, deep…"

RICHARD: *(Over this)* Marian, you okay?

(MARIAN nods.)

BENJAMIN: "I dress the perforated shoulder, the foot
  with bullet-wound,
Cleanse the one with the gnawing and putrid
  gangrene…I am faithful, I do not give out,
The fractur'd thigh, the knee, the wound in the
  abdomen, These and more I dress with impassive

hand (yet deep in my breast afire, a burning flame.)
Thus in silence in dreams' projections,
Returning, resuming, I thread my way through the
hospitals,
The hurt and wounded I pacify with soothing hand,
I sit by the restless all the dark night, some are so
young,
Some suffer so much...
I recall the experience—sweet and sad.
Many a soldier's loving arms about this neck have
cross'd and rested
Many a soldier's kiss dwells on these bearded lips."
(Then) Should I grow a beard?

(They laugh, she turns off the tape recorder.)

RICHARD: What's it called again?

BARBARA: *The Wound Dresser.*

JANE: If Benjamin were here, he'd be one of the most
vulnerable right now…

BARBARA: That's true…

JANE: So in a way it's a good thing…

BARBARA: I guess…I guess.

JANE: We pass by his grave in the cemetery on our
walks.

TIM: We do.

JANE: We always make sure we stop for a moment…

MARIAN: And Evan's?

JANE: At Evan's. We always stop there too.

(Lights fade.)

5.
Alone Together.

(The same, a short time later. In the middle of conversation:)

BARBARA: Still my turn... *(Then)* In the hospital. One of my nurses. She's Irish... She saw me listening to music on my smart phone... She'd always check: *(Irish accent)* 'what are you listening to—always the same thing, dear!' I love that accent. She'd make sure there was enough battery charge, so I could keep listening... In the midst of everything, she thought of that. *(Then)* She told me what she listens to—music her brother gave her. A jazz piece, she said it was called 'Alone Together.' Anyone know it?

JANE: Tim?

TIM: No.

BARBARA: On her breaks she'd listen, she said... *(To RICHARD)* Could you get me my phone...? In my jacket... In the hall hanging up...

(RICHARD goes off.)

JANE: Barbara, aren't you glad you finally got rid of your flip phone.

MARIAN: I never thought I'd see the day.

JANE: And joined the human race!

BARBARA: Is a smart phone what now defines the human race? I hope not...

(RICHARD returns with BARBARA's smart phone, and hands it to her.)

BARBARA: I'll play it and hold it up so you can hear... Marian you know this.

MARIAN: What is it?

BARBARA: You too Tim…

TIM: What??

BARBARA: We sang it in chorus at the Christmas concert. We've done it three times. Twice in the last two years. (*She scrolls through her smart phone.*)

RICHARD: This is what you played in the hospital.

BARBARA: I did…

RICHARD: Over and over again.

BARBARA: Yes. Here it is… Here. Everyone ready? (*She presses a button and she holds up the phone to the microphone on the computer.*)

(*Bach's* Mass In B Minor, Dona Nobis Pacem…)

MARIAN: A little louder, Barbara…

(BARBARA *turns up the volume.*)

BARBARA: Better?

(MARIAN *nods.*)

MARIAN: Of course, this. We sang this.

(*Music plays.*)

RICHARD: Is that your chorus singing?

BARBARA: No, we're not that good, Richard.

MARIAN: We wish…

(*Music continues.*)

BARBARA: (*To* RICHARD) Can you hold it?

(RICHARD *takes the smart phone and holds it up.*)

(*Music continues.*)

RICHARD: What is this piece?

MARIAN: If you'd come to our Christmas concert—.

TIM: Bach's *Mass in B Minor*, the *Dona Nobis Pacem*. 'Give us Peace'…

(Music continues.)

BARBARA: I thought I was going to die... *(Then)* I need to say that to you.

RICHARD: So did we, and I needed to say that...

(Music continues.)

BARBARA: That's enough.

(BARBARA *takes the smart phone and turns off the music.)*

BARBARA: I'm done, Richard. You can take that plate away.

RICHARD: You'll let me wait on you.

TIM: I'm finished too, Jane.

JANE: Just leave it. I don't want to touch your tray...

TIM: It'll smell up the room.

JANE: I'm not in there...

TIM: *(To the others)* She's joking...

RICHARD: *(To* BARBARA*)* You okay? You didn't eat much...

BARBARA: It was very good. Thank you...

(RICHARD *starts to pick up* BARBARA's *plate and take it off.)*

(No one knows what to say, then:)

BARBARA: Jane, Tim how are your kids?

RICHARD: *(Setting plate back down)* I want to hear this...

BARBARA: You talk to them?

TIM: All the time, Barbara...

JANE: Tim was just on the phone with Karen.

BARBARA: That's right. You said.

TIM: She's a senior. Like your students. She's upset. She's missing a lot. She's alone. She's stuck with her mom and step-dad. I think it's really hard when you're an only kid… It sucks.

MARIAN: Of course. It would be…

TIM: She says you can really hear the ambulances. Mostly in the night. There's little other traffic. It keeps her up… *(New subject:)* Billy's… You tell her, Jane.

JANE: Billy and his girlfriend are giving each other haircuts…

MARIAN: Have they sent pictures?

JANE: We've Skyped. *(She laughs.)*

TIM: They have a dog.

JANE: The dogs are so happy right now. Billy, remember started out of school in the recession, how hard that was? He's saying, 'here we go again'. 'Lucky me.' He's still pretty much low man on the totem pole in his office…

MARIAN: I talk to him.

JANE: I know you do.

BARBARA: Your son has already lost his job.

RICHARD: It was part time… He's just out of school.

BARBARA: He was going to go work in a grocery store…

JANE: Richard told us. Lily's doing well though, right?

RICHARD: Another year. We'll see what all of this is like then. Who the hell knows?

JANE: Barbara, the others know this, I told them—.

BARBARA: What?

JANE: Billy was upset the other day. He said he's just about had it with all this criticism of young people… You know, about them being cavalier, not caring, going to beaches. That's not what his friends see, he said.

His friends question how seriously their parents and grandparents have taken this.

RICHARD: The staying home, social distancing—?

JANE: *(Over this)* One of his friends speculated that older people, because they'd lived through, you know, possible nuclear war, because that never actually happened, so they think, too much is being made of this… That's what they see… *(Then)* This all just came out when I innocently said, 'Hey I think it's going to be all right.' 'You don't see,' he said and almost shouting at me, 'You don't really see how fragile things are… You don't see it through our eyes…'

(Then)

BARBARA: I know my students have felt that way… Feel that way. How it could all fall apart.

JANE: Billy's girlfriend, and she's really nice, I like her. She said to me— "it feels like the world is ending just as we are arriving."

(Then:)

BARBARA: I'm tired. Maybe we should stop…

RICHARD: I'll take your plate… *(He will take her plate to the kitchen.)*

JANE: How long have we been talking? *(Looks at her computer or phone)* My god…I thought you could only do forty minutes on Zoom before you have to pay. Did someone pay?

TIM: Richard was going to use his office account…

JANE: So we have Andrew Cuomo to thank for this too.

RICHARD: *(Returning)* We'll see. We'll see about that. Let's not go overboard about Andrew Cuomo…

BARBARA: What are you all going to do the rest of the night?

MARIAN: I know what I'm going to do.

BARBARA: What, Marian?

MARIAN: It's garbage night.

JANE: So?

MARIAN: A friend of mine sent me a You-Tube video—.

JANE: I get so many of those—.

TIM: Everyone does, Jane.

MARIAN: *(Continues)* Of a woman, she's carefully putting on makeup in front of a mirror. Lipstick. Blush… Then zipping herself up into a beautiful strappy dress, and then slipping into very high red heels, spike heels. She takes one more look in a full-length mirror now, smooths out the dress, goes to the front door, picks up a big bag of garbage, goes outside, and drops the garbage into the garbage can. And then goes back inside. That's me tonight. I'm going to get dressed up for garbage night. *(Then)* I need a cat…

JANE: We don't want to leave, Barbara…

RICHARD: *(Laughing)* We don't have anywhere to go…

TIM: I read somewhere, some writer, he said, 'you can't despair twenty-four hours a day.'

MARIAN: I'll write that out and put it on my fridge, Tim.

RICHARD: Come on, everyone, Barbara needs to rest…

JANE: Okay. Okay.

MARIAN: And Jane has grocery shopping to do…

JANE: Shut up… Okay, Richard.

MARIAN: Bye, Barbara. Goodnight. Thank God you're home… What a nightmare.

BARBARA: Goodnight.

MARIAN: Richard, Jane. Tim…

TIM: Marian, you still watching *Love Is Blind*?

MARIAN: Religiously, Tim... Thank you for suggesting it. Goodnight all. Goodnight... *(She signs off.)*

BARBARA: She seems good. Considering...

JANE: Considering that she's Marian?

BARBARA: Yeh.

TIM: Jane, I'm going to call Karen back...I said I'd do that...

JANE: Do it. Do it.

TIM: *(Over this)* She was upset...Barbara...Richard. 'Night.

RICHARD: Night.

BARBARA: Tim, how are you feeling?

(Then)

TIM: Better.

BARBARA: Take care of yourself.

TIM: I will.

BARBARA: Goodnight.

*(*TIM *signs off.)*

RICHARD: *(A joke)* Jane, I can't wait to do the dishes... *(He laughs.)* She *(*BARBARA*)* needs to go to bed...

JANE: I know. I know...

*(*RICHARD *goes off.)*

JANE: He's going to retire?

BARBARA: Sounds like it.

JANE: Is this the time to make such a decision?

BARBARA: I don't know. I don't know what I know... This was nice...

JANE: It was. Let's do it again. Tomorrow night?

BARBARA: Let's. That makes me happy. To know we'll do it again tomorrow... *(Then)* 'Night...

(JANE *signs off.*)

(BARBARA *alone.*)

(BARBARA *signs off.*)

END OF PLAY